What Makes a Family?

All Kinds of Families

by Martha E. H. Rustad

Pebble Plus is published by Pebble
1710 Roe Crest Drive,
North Mankato, Minnesota 56003
www.mycapstone.com

Library of Congress Cataloging-in-Publication Data
Library of Congress Cataloging-in-Publication Data is available on the Library of Congress website.
ISBN 978-1-9771-0902-6 (library binding)
ISBN 978-1-9771-1054-1 (paperback)
ISBN 978-1-9771-1272-9 (eBook PDF)

Editorial Credits
Marissa Kirkman, editor; Cynthia Della-Rovere, designer;
Eric Gohl, media researcher; Tori Abraham, production specialist

Image Credits
iStockphoto: Aleksandar Nakic, cover, ferrantraite, 9; Shutterstock: absolute-india, 17, imtmphoto, 11, In The Light Photography, 7, India Picture, 19, Monkey Business Images, 21, Mr.Whiskey, 1, VGstockstudio, 13, wavebreakmedia, 5, 15
Design Elements: Shutterstock

All internet sites appearing in back matter were available and accurate when this book was sent to press.

Note to Parents and Teachers
The What Makes a Family? set supports national standards related to social studies. This book describes and illustrates different kinds of families. The images support early readers in understanding the text. The repetition of words and phrases helps early readers learn new words. This book also introduces early readers to subject-specific vocabulary words, which are defined in the Glossary section. Early readers may need assistance to read some words and to use the Table of Contents, Glossary, Read More, Internet Sites, Critical Thinking Questions, and Index sections of the book.

Printed and bound in China.
001654

Table of Contents

What Is a Family?

This is my family! We take care of each other. We like to be together. My family shares a home and lots of love.

Every family looks different.

Some families are big.

Others are small. All families

are important.

People in a Family

This family has two dads and two kids. They make a meal together. Dad cuts vegetables. Big sister, Maria, helps. Mateo and Papa make a salad.

This family has a dad, one kid, and two grandparents. After school, Grandma helps Henry with homework. Then Grandpa and Henry play a game.

This family has a dad, a
stepmom, and three stepsiblings.
They clean together. Big brother,
Luke, vacuums. Luke's stepmom
irons clothes. His sisters help.

This family has two foster parents and two kids. A child lives with foster parents when her own parents cannot care for her. This family watches a movie.

Families Love Each Other

This family has an aunt, an uncle, and four kids. Joe's parents are in the military. His aunt and uncle take care of him while his parents are away.

This family has one parent and one child. They tell each other about their days. They talk about both good and bad events. Mom hugs Hemant.

No two families are the same.

Families take care of each other.

They love each other. We need

our families!

Glossary

aunt—the sister of a person's mother or father; an aunt also can be the wife of a person's uncle

brother—a male sibling

dad—a male parent

foster parent—an adult who cares for a child when the child's other family members cannot

grandma—the mother of a person's mother or father

grandpa—the father of a person's mother or father

mom—a female parent

sister—a female sibling

stepmom—a woman who marries a person's parent after the death or divorce of the person's mother

stepsibling—a brother or sister who is added to your family when your mom or dad gets remarried

uncle—the brother of a person's mother or father; an uncle also can be the husband of a person's aunt

Read More

Cavell-Clarke, Steffi. *Different Families.* New York: Crabtree Publishing Company, 2018.

Harrington, Claudia. *My Two Moms.* My Family. Minneapolis: Looking Glass Library, 2016.

Raatma, Lucia. *Brothers Are Part of a Family.* Our Families. North Mankato, MN: Capstone Press, 2018.

Internet Sites

Fun Family Activities
http://www.childfun.com/themes/people/families/

Make a Printable Book about Your Family
http://printables.atozteacherstuff.com/download/book_family_all.pdf

Make a Family Tree
https://family-tree-template.org/wp-content/uploads/2012/12/family-tree-with-red-leaves.jpg

Critical Thinking Questions

1. How is your family like other families? How is it different?

2. What is an uncle? (Use the glossary for help.)

3. What is your favorite activity to do with your family?

Index